THE FEAR OF
GOD

THE FEAR OF
GOD

STEPHEN C. YOHN

WESTBOW
PRESS®
A DIVISION OF THOMAS NELSON
& ZONDERVAN

WestBow Press books may be ordered through booksellers or by contacting:

WestBow Press
A Division of Thomas Nelson & Zondervan
1663 Liberty Drive
Bloomington, IN 47403
www.westbowpress.com
1 (866) 928-1240

Scripture taken from the New King James Version®. Copyright © 1982 by Thomas Nelson. Used by permission. All rights reserved.

ISBN: 978-1-9736-1522-4 (sc)
ISBN: 978-1-9736-1521-7 (hc)
ISBN: 978-1-9736-1523-1 (e)

Library of Congress Control Number: 2018900537

Print information available on the last page.

WestBow Press rev. date: 1/25/2018

To my wife Brenda who was supportive of my attempt to write on this difficult subject, because she too is a believer in the fear of God.

I would like to thank David Nealon (recently deceased) who was a good friend and a constant encouragement for me to write. D.C. Lundy was also one who encouraged me to write as we served together in his ministry in Uganda, Africa called "Kingdom Works Ministries International." Finally, my brother Jim Yohn, who during many phone calls gently prodded me to write.

Contents

PART 3. LET'S REVIEW

PART 1

The Fear of God:
Definitions, Explanations,
and Answers

INTRODUCTION

RECENTLY, ON A PUBLIC BROADCASTING STATION, a wedding was being held at a local Portland, Oregon, donut shop. In keeping with the city's self-description, which was, "Keep Portland weird," Portland once again succeeded by celebrating this donut-shop wedding. The camera panned the shop as many indulged in its fare (I can only imagine shaking hands with someone who had just finished a jelly donut). Then a local minister arrived to perform the ceremony. After the nuptials had been completed, the groom wiped off some extra powdered sugar from his lower lip and kissed his bride.

The PBS reporter asked the so-called minister if this was an appropriate place for a wedding. The minister then began to gush something about his God being a god of joy and celebration while he waved his arms in the air, had a large grin, and looked heavenward. He continued to blather that God loved celebrations, even donut-shop weddings. If anyone had objected, I'm sure he would have condemned that person as being a donut-hating, whole-food advocate.

My objection to this wedding was with the minister and his

theology and not the marriage. He was implying that anyone who didn't share his myopic view of God was wrong. I protest! I don't share his view. How did he know that God was a god of joy and celebration? Is God only one-dimensional? Does anyone of sound mind really believe that God is a god of celebration only? Does this square with the world of suffering we observe on a daily basis? This religious person wanted to believe this about God and dismiss everything else the Bible declares about him.

Many years ago, in my sociology class, the professor invited a homosexual to come and speak to us about homosexuality. The speaker then talked for about thirty minutes and after that, allowed a time for questions. One lady raised her hand and asked him about the biblical passages that condemn homosexuality, to which he answered, "I don't believe that. My God is a god of love who accepts everyone." Again, here is a person who wants to believe something about God and dismisses all other declarations about God. Limiting God to what we want to believe about him is a very convenient way to justify ourselves.

What we need is for God to send us someone who can tell us about God. That was precisely what God did when he sent Christ. The Bible says, "For God did not send his Son into the world to condemn the world, but that the world through him might be saved" (John 3:17). Jesus affirmed this when he said, "No one has ascended to heaven but he who came down from heaven, that is the Son of Man (Jesus Christ), who is in heaven"(John 3:13). Here Christ makes it clear that no one has gone to heaven and returned to tell us about it except Christ because heaven was and is his home. Later Jesus said, "I speak what I've seen with my Father," and, "But now you seek to kill me, a Man who has told you the truth which I heard from God" (John 8:38, 40).

Listen to what Christ, the Son of man and of God, who was sent by God to us, declared about the fear of God. He said:

> "Whatever I tell you in the dark, speak in the light; and what you hear in the ear, preach on the house tops. And do not fear those who kill the body but cannot kill the soul. But rather fear him (God) who is able to destroy both soul and body in hell" (Matthew 10:27–28).

CHAPTER 1

Solomon, One of the Wisest Men Who Ever Lived,
Came to the Same Conclusion as Christ

WE READ IN ECCLESIASTES 12:13–14, "LET US HEAR the conclusion of the whole matter: 'Fear God and keep his commandments, for this is man's all. For God will bring every work into judgment. Including every secret thing. Whether good or evil!" Solomon reached this conclusion through a process of trial and error. He started out on the right foot by taking heed of his father's admonition. King David said to him,

> Now, my son, may the Lord be with you; and may you prosper, and build the house of the Lord your God, as he said to you. Only may he give you wisdom and understanding, and give you charge of Israel, that you may keep the law of the Lord your God. Then you will prosper, if you take care to fulfill the statutes and judgments with which the Lord charged Moses concerning Israel. Be strong and of good courage; do not fear or be dismayed (1 Chronicles 22:11–13).

Solomon's quest for wisdom began with a prayer. After David's death, Solomon became king over Israel.

> God appeared to Solomon and said to him, "Ask! What shall I give you? And Solomon said to God: You have shown great mercy to David my father, and have made me king in his place. Now, Oh Lord God, let your promise to David my father be established, for you have made me king over a people like the dust of the earth in multitude. Now give me wisdom and knowledge that I may go out and come in before this people; for who can judge this great people of yours? Then God said to Solomon: Because this was in your heart, and you have not asked for riches or wealth or honor, or the life of your enemies, nor have you asked for long life—but have asked for wisdom and knowledge for yourself, that you may judge my people over whom I have made you king—wisdom and knowledge are granted to you; and I will give you riches and wealth and honor, such as none of the kings have had who were before you, nor shall any after you have the like" (2 Chronicles 1:7–12).

Seeing the enormous challenges that lay ahead of him and following his father David's admonition to get wisdom and understanding from the Lord, Solomon began his reign with prayer. However, Solomon fell short of the second admonition, which was to "keep the law of the Lord your God and fulfill the statutes and judgments which the Lord charged Moses" (1 Chronicles 22:13). His failure to fear God and keep his commandments would undermine his reputation and legacy.

Earlier in his life, he wrote proverbs and compiled them into the book of the Bible called Proverbs. At this point in his life, he could determine what was wise and what was foolish, simply by contrast and comparison. But later in his life, he would learn what was foolish by participating in foolishness. The result was that he compromised his faith and understanding. Watch his downward spiral unfold.

> I said in my heart, Come now, I will test you with mirth, therefore enjoy pleasure; but surely, this also was vanity. I said of laughter—madness! And of pleasure, what does it accomplish? I searched in my heart how to gratify my flesh with wine, while guiding my heart with wisdom, and how to lay hold on folly; till I might see what was good for the sons of men to do under heaven all the days of their lives.

> I made my works great, I built myself houses, and planted myself vineyards. I made myself gardens and orchards, and I planted all kinds of fruit trees in them. I made for myself water pools from which to water the growing trees of the grove. I acquired male and female servants, and had servants born in my house. Yes, I had greater possessions of herds and flocks that all who were in Jerusalem before me. I also gathered for myself silver and gold and the special treasures of kings and provinces. I acquired male and female singers, the delights of the sons of men, and musical instruments of all kinds (Ecclesiastes 2:4–8).

We can also read of Solomon's failure to fear God and keep his commandments.

> So I became great and excelled more than all who were before me in Jerusalem. Also my wisdom remained with me. Whatever my eyes desired I did not keep from them. I did not withhold my heart from any pleasure, for my heart rejoiced in all my labor; and this was my reward for all my labor. Then I looked on all the works my hands had done and on the labor in which I had toiled; and indeed all was vanity (meaningless) and grasping for the wind. There was no profit under the sun (Ecclesiastes 2:1–11).

Two other passages in the Bible give us insight into Solomon. While he was certainly wealthy, successful, and powerful, the things that enticed him the most subverted his heart. Here is the first.

> But King Solomon loved many foreign women, as well as the daughter of Pharaoh: women of the Moabites, Ammonites, Edomites, Sidonians, and Hittites—from the nations from whom the Lord said to the children of Israel, you shall not intermarry with them, nor they with you. Surely they will turn away your hearts after other gods. Solomon clung to these in love. And he had seven hundred wives, princesses, and three hundred concubines; and his wives turned away his heart. For it was so when, Solomon was old, that his wives turned his heart after other gods; and his heart was not loyal to the Lord his God, as was the heart of his father David. For Solomon went after Ashtoreth the goddess of the Sidonians (the goddess of love and fertility), and after Milcom (Milcom/Molech who demanded the sacrifice of children by burning them to death) the abomination of the Ammonites. Solomon did evil in the sight of the Lord, and did not fully follow the Lord, as did his father David. Then Solomon built a high place for Chemosh, the abomination of Moab, on a hill east of Jerusalem and for Molech the abomination of the people of Ammon. And he did likewise for all his foreign wives, who burned incense and sacrificed to their gods. So the Lord became angry with Solomon, because his heart had turned from the Lord God of Israel, who had appeared to him twice, and had commanded him concerning this thing, that he should not go after other gods; but he did not keep what the Lord had commanded. Therefore the Lord said to Solomon, because you have done this, and have not kept my covenant and my statutes, which I have commanded you, I will surely tear the kingdom away from you and give it to your servant (1 Kings 11:1–11).

The next insight we get from Solomon is found in Ecclesiastes 7:25–26.

> I applied my heart to know, to search and seek out wisdom and the reason of things, to know wickedness and folly, even of foolishness and madness. And I find, more bitter than death the woman whose heart is snares and nets, whose hands are fetters. He who pleases God shall escape from her, but the sinner will be trapped by her.

What happens to people who indulge all of their passions and appetites? They become slaves to these passions and appetites. These passions and appetites begin to rule over people so that they can't do the right and good thing. It doesn't matter whether or not these people are religious. When individuals give in to the passions of their minds and imaginations and the desires of their bodies, these passions and desires will grow stronger and stronger until they rule over these individuals. In our day and age, we no longer use the term *slavery* but rather *addiction*. In either case, we've created a situation where we cannot always do the right thing.

This is what Solomon did. He indulged the passions of his mind, imagination, eyes, and body. He said, "Whatever my eyes desired I did not keep from them. I did not withhold my heart from any pleasure" (Ecclesiastes 2:10). He goes on to confess, "I applied my heart to know, to search and seek out wisdom and the reason of things, to know wickedness and folly, even foolishness and madness" (Ecclesiastes 7:25–26).

What was the net effect of those things on his life?

> "So the Lord became angry with Solomon, because his heart had turned from the Lord God of Israel, who had appeared to him twice, and had commanded him concerning this

thing, that he should not go after other gods; but he did not keep what the Lord had commanded him. Therefore, the Lord said to Solomon, because you have done this, and have not kept my covenant and my statutes, which I have commanded you, I will surely tear the kingdom away from you and give it to your servant." (1 Kings 11:9–11)

As incredible as this may sound, Solomon said, "Also my wisdom remained with me" (Ecclesiastes 2:9). This was true only because "the gifts and the calling of God are irrevocable" (Romans 11:29). In other words, God's gift of wisdom to Solomon was not conditional but was an actual gift from God, no matter what Solomon decided to do with it.

We know that Solomon's gift of wisdom remained with him until the end of his life because of his conclusion in the book of Ecclesiastes. He said, "Let us hear the sum of the whole matter: Fear God and keep his commandments, for this is man's all. For God will bring every work into judgment, including every secret thing, whether good or evil" (Ecclesiastes 12:13–14). "For this is man's all" means that there is nothing more significant we can do with our lives than fear God and keep his commandments in light of God's impending judgment.

Whatever we pursue in life, we, like Solomon, will consider our lives to have been vain because our lives are so short. The human life span is compared to a mist or a vapor, which briefly makes an appearance and then disappears and is gone. Not only is this life span short in length and fleeting, but it begins with a fifteen- to twenty-year growth and development period and ends with a final ten to twenty years of decline in health, presuming an individual doesn't die prematurely from something unexpected.

Solomon also highlighted the meaninglessness of our lives. He observed that we might be rich or poor, wise or foolish, talented or lacking talent. We might have good or bad circumstances or health, but we all come to the same end and die after very short lives. He used people's occupations as his example. We work hard all of our lives, save, and gather possessions, and then we die and leave everything behind. To whom do we leave it all? Will it be a foolish person, who will waste all that we have left? Or a stingy person, who will help no one? Or a wise person, who will build up what we have left and ensure our legacies? We don't know! This is just another example of the meaninglessness of our lives and unanswered and unanswerable questions we all have (see Ecclesiastes 2:18).

John MacArthur observed in his commentary on the book of Ecclesiastes and wrote,

> While the context in each case will determine which meaning Solomon is focusing on (life is fleeting, meaningless or incomprehensible), the most recurring theme is incomprehensible or unknowable, referring to the mysteries of God's purposes. Solomon's conclusion "to fear God and keep his commandments" is more than the books summary; it is the only hope of the good life and the only reasonable response of faith and obedience to sovereign God. He (God) precisely works out all activities under the sun, each in its time according his perfect plan, but also discloses only as much as his perfect wisdom dictates and holds all men accountable. Those who refuse to take God and his Word seriously are doomed to live lives of the severest vanity."[1]

God will bring all that we've done and said into judgment. Because of this, we should fear him. This, as you can imagine, isn't a popular topic. As I mentioned earlier, people do not want a God who has standards, who is multidimensional in his personality, and who will judge them and hold them personally accountable for how they have lived their lives. Instead, they want to believe that God is only one-dimensional and is a god of love only, who will warmly welcome all into heaven without any condemnation or judgment. This is nonsense! Does a one-dimensional god of love square with reality as we know it?

Augustine, in the third century, painted a grim picture of the human condition, and it hasn't changed in seventeen hundred years. He wrote,

> As for that first origin of mankind, this present life of ours (if a state so full of grievous misery can be called a life) is evidence that all the mortal descendants of the first man came under condemnation. What else is the message of all the evils of humanity? The love of futile and harmful satisfactions with the results: worrisome anxieties, agitations of mind, disappointments, fears, frenzied joys, quarrels, disputes, wars, treacheries, hatreds, enmities, deceits, flattery, fraud, theft, plunder, betrayal, pride, ambition, envy, murder, killing of parents, cruelty, savagery, villainy, lust, promiscuity, indecency, un-chastity, fornication, adultery, incest, unnatural vice in men and women, sacrilege, collusion, false witness, unjust judgment, violence, robbery, and all other such evils, which do not immediately come to mind, although they never cease to beset this life of man – all these evils belong to man in his wickedness, and they all spring from that root of error and perverted affection which every son of Adam brings with him at his birth.[2]

We could add to this list such problems that come with marriages, children, step families, emotions, toxic behaviors (drugs and alcohol), work, relationships, money, and health (endless medical tests and medications). I'm sure the reader could add more.

Doesn't this sound familiar? Doesn't this sound like our day and age? Doesn't this sound like the history of the world, from its beginning all the way down to us? The only differences are scale and information. The scale of the twenty-first century far exceeds the third century because our populations are so much larger. Information on the evils of this world are placed before us on a daily basis.

Where do we see the love of God in this world? I would argue that we seldom see it—even from the Christian who is under Christ's command to "love one another and our neighbor." From them, we might see small demonstrations of love and common courtesy, such as letting someone go before them, holding a door open, giving someone a word of encouragement or a compliment, lending a helping hand, alternating between love and anger toward their children, and even occasionally, turning the other cheek and not returning evil for evil. There are also Christian missions that do works of charity during natural disasters, build hospitals and schools, treat the sick or injured, run adoption agencies, and offer emergency assistance.

While all of these things are commendable and a testimony of God's love, we don't see these things unless they are placed before us. Instead, the reality that we most often know is a world of evil placed before us to read, watch, and listen to by all forms of media on a daily basis. Why is this so? Because we live in a world that is full of suffering, pain, and death, and most often, this is the reality of life we experience.

The greatest act of God's love that we have ever seen was when God allowed Christ to be put to death. We're told,

> "For when we were still without strength (helpless), in due time Christ died for the ungodly. For scarcely for a righteous man will one die; yet perhaps for a good man someone would even dare to die. But God demonstrates

his own love toward us, in that while we were still sinners, Christ died for us" (Romans 5:6–8).

This is significant because we were incapable of helping ourselves, so God took the initiative, even though we, as sinners, were openly hostile to him. This act of God emanated from his character of love and not from finding anything desirable in us. As a result, his love has impacted millions of people, down through the ages, through his church. In fact, we only know what the true nature of love is because of the sacrificial death of Christ on our behalf (see 1 John 3:16). Apart from this, the love that we do encounter in this world is small by comparison and likely to come from merely a nice person.

Chapter 2

*Failure to Fear God and Keep His Commandments
Will Result in a Predictable Consequence*

THE PREDICTABLE CONSEQUENCE WOULD BE THAT people would do what is right in their own eyes.

Could any human society survive if its citizens did what was right in their own eyes? I suppose a small nation could if it had a true libertarian government and a populace that believed in full, individual freedom of thought, expression, and action, but no nation could dismiss the laws of the land and survive. A consensus would have to be reached by a majority of people, or it would soon descend into anarchy and chaos and then be forced to establish new laws to provide stability and security.

Doing what is right in our own eyes will never work. Likewise, we can't dismiss God's direction in the bible without serious ramifications. He gave his law to us so we could live together and before God in peace.

> "All scripture is given by inspiration of God, and is profitable for doctrine, for reproof (rebuke for wrong behavior, or belief), for correction, for instruction in righteousness, that

the man of God may be complete, thoroughly equipped for every good work" (2 Timothy 3:16).

Does this sound like we're free to do whatever is right in our own eyes? No, it doesn't. Rather, it sounds like we've been given concrete and sound direction on how to live with our fellow humans as well as God. We see this played out in the book of Psalms.

"How can a young man cleanse his way? By taking heed according to your word. With my whole heart I have sought you; oh, let me not wander from your commandments! Your word have I hidden in my heart that I might not sin against you" (Psalm 119:9–11).

Here, the psalmist's concern is how to live righteously before God. Is this something that also concerns those who seek to do whatever is right in their own eyes? No, it is irrelevant to them, because it doesn't square with what they want to believe about God.

The psalmist continues to show us that we need the illumination and direction of God's Word, laws, and commandments, without which we will continue to stumble along in this world, wondering what tripped us up.

"Your word is a lamp unto my feet and a light to my path" (Psalm 119:105).

This is how Solomon was able to conclude that we should fear God and keep his commandments.

Doing what is right in our own eyes begins with self-justification. Self-justification has its roots in pride and a belief in one's own goodness. This afflicts the rich most often. In fact, many cultures, down through history, believed that God blessed the rich, otherwise, they wouldn't be rich. Some of the rich thought they were rich because of their goodness. It's hard to argue against this because the rich aren't generally crude or involved in petty crime but are better educated and live in areas insulated from crime. Hence their miscalculation leads them to the wrong conclusion about themselves.

On the other hand, the poor are involved in self-justification by excusing themselves and arguing that they are what they are because of what others have done to them. They feel disenfranchised and excluded from opportunities, which the rich don't suffer from. This is true to some degree. So they are what they are because of what others have done to them.

In fact, people in all classes participate in self-justification, which is an exaggerated opinion of oneself, whether good or bad, right or wrong, or true or false. Without the guidance of the Word of God, we'll all end up doing what is right in our own eyes. We will then begin to excuse the way we are. I was born this way. I was raised this way. I am what I am because of what others have done to me. My environment shaped me. The culture of the time shaped my worldview. I had few opportunities. I was abused emotionally or physically. On and on the list of excuses grow as we reflect on our lives. The fascinating thing about all of the above excuses is that they are all true to some degree in everyone.

Jesus, however, was compassionate concerning legitimate excuses but exposed and dismissed weak and insincere ones that people made to avoid what he had to say. He did so with a short story.

> He said: "A certain man gave a great supper and invited many, and sent his servant at supper time to say to those who were invited, come, for all things are now ready. But they all with one accord began to make excuses. The first

said to him, I have bought a piece of ground, and I must go and see it. I ask you to have me excused. And another said, I have bought five yoke of oxen, and I am going to test them. I ask you to have me excused. Still another said I have married a wife, and therefore I cannot come. So that servant came and reported these things to his master. Then the master of the house, being angry, said to his servant, go out quickly into the streets and lanes of the city, and bring in here the poor, and the maimed, the lame, and the blind. And the servant said, master it is done as you have commanded, and still there is room. Then the master said to the servant, go out into the highways and hedges, and compel them to come in, that my house may be filled. For I say to you that none of those men who were invited shall taste my supper" (Luke 14:16–24).

The first three people represent those who were known by their master. Although very polite, they made it clear they weren't interested by making lame excuses. Who buys land without first looking at it? Who would buy farm animals without first examining them? The newlyweds offered no excuse but implied it wasn't convenient for them. The second group, made up of the poor and less fortunate, also made excuses for not being able to attend. We see this by a third invitation that was given and extended to the lowest class of people. Even then, not all of them came.

Self-deception lies behind the failure to fear God and keep his commandments. This is observed in the psalms: "For the wicked boasts of his heart's desire. He blesses the greedy and renounces the Lord. The wicked in his proud countenance does not seek God. God is in none of his thoughts. He has said in his heart, God has forgotten; He hides his face; He will never see" (Psalm 10:3–4, 11).

Those who have dismissed God from their lives, whose unbelief has blinded their eyes, and who hold only to the natural order, may come to the above conclusions. Such people do not have God in their thoughts, unless it is to renounce God and deny that they will ever be held accountable for their lives. They also conclude that because God's judgment is deferred instead of immediate, then judgment is nothing more than religious control to keep the masses of people in line. Instead of recognizing God's mercy, compassion, and patience, which allow for the repentance and the restoration of failed people, they see the delay as an opportunity to commit more evil (see Ecclesiastes 8:11).

While judgment is often deferred, giving the appearance that someone is getting away with evil and even allowing others to further disobey, it in no way impacts the final decision by God where perfect, complete, and eternal judgment will be rendered to all. For the time being, God commands everyone everywhere to repent.

The apostle Paul gives us this warning,

> I charge you [Timothy] therefore before God and the Lord Jesus Christ, who will judge the living and the dead at his appearing and his kingdom: Preach the word! Be ready in season and out of season. Convince, rebuke, exhort, with all longsuffering and teaching. For the time will come when they will not endure sound doctrine, but according to their own desires, because they have itching ears, they will heap up for themselves teachers; and they will turn their ears away from the truth, and be turned aside to fables. But you be watchful in all things, endure afflictions, do the work of an evangelist, fulfill your ministry. (2 Timothy 4:1–5)

John MacArthur comments on this passage in 2 Timothy 4:3 and writes,

Many people would become intolerant of the confrontive demanding preaching of God's Word. This will result in itching ears. These are people who follow their own desires and flock to preachers who offer them God's blessing apart from his forgiveness and salvation, apart from their repentance. They have an itch to be entertained by teachings that will produce pleasant sensations and leave them with good feelings about themselves. Their goal is that men preach according to their own desires. Under those conditions, people will dictate what men preach, rather than God dictating it by his Word.

The consequence of men defaulting back to doing what is right in their own eyes confirms the proverb, "As a dog returns to its own vomit, so a fool repeats his folly" (Proverbs 26:11).

CHAPTER 3

What Is the Fear of God?

Four Ways to Define the Fear of the Lord

SOLOMON DESCRIBES THE FEAR OF GOD IN FOUR different ways.

1. The Fear of the Lord is the Beginning of Knowledge

The first is this: "The fear of the Lord is the beginning of knowledge" (Proverbs 1:7). This knowledge isn't a scientific principle gleaned from the experiment and observation of the natural world. Rather, as John Macarthur wrote,

> (Biblical knowledge) deals with practical righteousness, by addressing man's ethical choices, calling into question how he thinks, lives, manages his daily life in light of divine truth. More specifically, Proverbs calls man to live as the creator intended him to live when he made man.[3]

Again, "Biblical knowledge deals with practical righteousness." In other words, how do we live in right relationship with God? We live in right relationship with God by faith, which is the most logical thing we can do. Since God is infinite and we are finite, faith is essential. What can we understand about him? Nothing, except that which he has disclosed to us about himself, because God cannot be observed or measured as the natural world can. This isn't blind faith but one that has internal coherence and a logic that appeals to our reason.

For instance, the Bible tells us, "Since the creation of the world his invisible attributes (God's) are clearly seen, being understood by the things that are made, even his eternal power and Godhead" (Romans 1:20). We see that the created order, whether it is under the power of a microscope or a telescope, sends a clear message about God. In this case, it's a message about his eternal power. Anyone who could speak the created order into existence possesses awesome and omnipotent power.

The second thing that is revealed about God from the natural order is his Godhead. This is his divine nature, which stands outside of and is external from the natural order. We actually learn something about the character of God from the natural order of the world and the universe. We specifically learn about the goodness of God from these things. God, himself, bears witness that he is good.

The Bible says, "He (God) did not leave himself without a witness, in that he did good, and gave us rain from heaven, and fruitful seasons, filling our hearts with food and gladness" (Acts 14:17). God's witness of himself, through his eternal power and divine nature, is aimed at man's reason. This culminates in "the fear of the Lord being the beginning of knowledge" (Proverbs 1:7)—knowledge of God, the universe, and ourselves.

Not only does God appeal to man's reason through the created order but also through direct commands on how we are to live, think, and manage our daily lives. God calls man to live as he (the Creator) intended us to live. He did this through the Ten Commandments.

> You shall have no other gods before me, don't worship idols, don't take the name of the Lord your God in vain, keep the Sabbath, honor your father and mother, do not murder, do not commit adultery, don't steal, don't lie or bear false witness, and do not envy. (Exodus 20:1–17)

Christ adds something to the commandments when he says, "Love God with all of your heart, soul, mind, and strength, and love your neighbor as yourself" (Matthew 22:37–40). This is how God always intended us to live. The beginning of knowledge and the fear of God come when we understand his commands for us.

2. The Fear of the Lord Is to Hate Evil

> The fear of the Lord is to hate evil. (Proverbs 8:13)

There are things that God hates, even though some people don't want to believe that about him. We would be wise to hate the same things he does.

> There are six things the Lord hates, yes, seven are an abomination to him: a proud look, a lying tongue, hands that shed innocent blood, a heart that devises wicked plans, feet that are swift in running to evil, a false witness who speaks lies, and one who sows discord among brethren. (Proverbs 6:16–19)

The numbers six and seven are used to get our attention. They are not meant to be an exhaustive list but to shock our understanding of the theological truth that there are things that God hates. Again, this truth needs to be underscored because there are people who don't want to believe this about God. There are things that God hates.

Surely some sentimental person will say, "I don't believe that. My God is a god of love." Which position is true: what one person wants to believe about God or what God has disclosed about himself? What we choose to believe is merely our opinion—one among billions of opinions—unless our opinion reflects the self-disclosure God has made about himself.

Here is another surprising belief people have: Man is basically good. Those who hold this opinion believe that we make mistakes but can correct our mistakes and make many wrong choices in life but can overcome these by making good choices. They also believe that we live in an environment that promotes bad habits and bad choices and that economic inequality forms wrong mind-sets that we act out against to defend ourselves from oppressive systems.

They who hold these views believe that education will eliminate and correct all of these flaws in us. I, too, believe that man can improve his lot in life through good, sound, moral and ethical choices, but I do not believe that man is basically good or that we will see this played out before us more than occasionally. Instead, we see the things that God hates cross all economic and educational barriers. These things have been with us throughout recorded history, and no man has overcome them by use of government, educational system, or individual initiative.

Man is not basically good but rather basically bad in the core of his being. The Bible calls him a sinner. He is so conflicted that when he wants to do what is good and right, he can't, and when he wants to abstain from evil, that is the very thing he does. Why? It's because of the sin within him (see Romans 7:19).

The only way out for us is through a deep and sincere repentance, without which, we will be unable to renovate our lives. True repentance can only proceed from a sincere fear of God, which brings us to a point where we hate what God hates. The Bible says that it is, "by the fear of the Lord that one departs from evil" (Proverbs 16:6).

I don't think that evil resonates with most people. Some may think that there are and have been evil people throughout history, but they don't think of themselves as evil. From that point of view, it is easy for them to believe that because someone may not be involved in gross evil, such as murder, kidnapping, sexual exploitation, war mongering, dealing drugs, stealing, or whatever gross evil one can think of, they are excused from being evil.

I place myself in this category. I do not think of myself as being evil but rather as one who has many weaknesses to which I regularly yield. This frequently makes my behavior problematic but not in the category of monstrous evil. Yet the Lord Christ charged us *all* with being evil. He said,

> If you then, being evil, know how to give good gifts to your children, how much more will your Father who is in heaven give good things to those who ask him. (Matthew 7:11)

Here, the Lord brings forward the paradox of us being evil and at the same time, being capable of doing good deeds. Christ presupposes human depravity when he says, "If you then, being evil." It is an unequivocal charge. Even if we're not involved in any gross evil, we can still do what is moral and ethical, as indicated by Christ's words about us giving good things to our children.

Augustine, a third-century bishop in North Africa, gave us great insight into the concept of evil.

When an evil choice happens in any being, then what happens is dependent on the will of that being; the failure is voluntary, not necessary, and the punishment that follows is just. For this failure does not consist in defection to things which are evil in themselves; it is the defection itself that is evil. That is, it is not a falling away to evil natures; the defection is evil in itself, as a defection from him who supremely exists to something of a lower degree of reality; and this is contrary to the order of nature.

Greed, for example, is not something wrong with gold; the fault is in a man who perversely loves gold and for its sake abandons justice, which ought to be put beyond comparison above gold. Lust is not something wrong in a beautiful and attractive body; the fault is in a soul which perversely delights in sensual pleasures, to the neglect of that self-control by which we are made fit for spiritual realities far more beautiful, with a loveliness which cannot fade.

There is then no efficient natural or (if we may so call it) essential cause of evil choice, since the evil of mutable spirits arises from the evil choice, and that evil diminishes and corrupts the goodness of nature. And this evil choice consists solely in falling away from God and deserting him, a defection whose cause is deficient, in the sense of being wanting—for there is no cause.[4]

Therefore, we are all evil in the sense that we have defected from God through unbelief. We have chosen to love and be devoted to things that are temporal and mutable, which by their own definitions cannot bring us happiness because they are temporal and change. Only God is eternal and unchangeable, and it is only here that we can find peace, joy, happiness, and satisfaction. Only God can provide these things forever because only he is eternal and unchanging. All other things are good in their proper places, but when we seek them in place of God, it will only result in misery—the very thing we see taking place in the world—because such choices are contrary to the order of nature. If we want to depart from evil then we must return to God, who is the greatest good, and quit looking for happiness in things that cannot make us happy.

3. The Fear of the Lord Is a Fountain of Life

> The fear of the Lord is a fountain of life, to turn one away
> from the snares of death. (Proverbs 14:27)

This truth comes to us through God's self-disclosure. If we don't embrace it as such, we will default to doing what is right in our own eyes through trial and error or by embracing the makeshift philosophies of popular wisdom, which are always available where men defect from faith in God.

Man needs the guidance of our Creator since he alone designed us and knows what will make us happy. He alone knows how he constructed us emotionally, psychologically, physically, and spiritually.

What does an emotionally healthy person look like? It is a person who loves the praise of God more than the praise of others. Such people can rest in God's praise and affirmation, knowing that they have done the right thing. On the other hand, people who love the praise of others more than the praise of God are emotionally unhealthy since they seek affirmation from a lesser good and will eventually compromise their consciences in order to maintain the status quo, no matter how wrong that might be.

A psychologically healthy person directs his or her life by God's self-disclosure in Christ. This individual does so by following Christ and keeping his commandments. This person will never be satisfied until he or she measures up to the full stature of Christ. This individual will succeed because this is God's will and the choice to do so is sanctioned by God.

Likewise, we gradually begin to treat our bodies the way God designed them to be treated. Our bodies are not ours to do with as we wish. We're not to commit the sins of gluttony, sexual immorality, indolence, or ingesting toxic substances that impair us to a point where we hurt ourselves or someone else.

We're told that when we align ourselves with the fear of God, our lives will actually be prolonged. We will live longer when our lives are directed by the Word of God (see Proverbs 10:27). We will still die, but we'll be spared the consequences of the person who reaps what he or she sows in rebellion against God. This will happen naturally because, "The fear of the Lord leads to life, and he who has it will abide in satisfaction; he will not be visited with evil" (Proverbs 19:23).

4. The Fear of the Lord Is the Beginning of Wisdom

> The fear of the Lord is the beginning of wisdom, and the knowledge of the holy one is understanding. For by me your days will be multiplied, and the years of life will be added to you. If you are wise, you will be wise for yourself, and if you scoff, you will bear it alone. (Proverbs 9:10–12)

Here we see responsibility thrust upon us by God. We are responsible for the choices we make and the direction our lives go. We can choose to follow the wisdom that fears God or to scoff in unbelief. We will move in one direction or the other and will bear the consequences alone.

Chapter 4

We Should Fear God Because He Will Judge Us

Again, we learn about Solomon's conclusion on life when he says, "Fear God and keep his commandments, for this is man's all. For God will bring every work into judgment. Including, every secret thing, whether good or evil" (Ecclesiastes 12:13–14).

Why do people have such a hard time with God judging us? Isn't judgment a daily reality for us? Don't we all participate in and render judgment over politics, government leaders, employers, jobs, policies, world conditions, weather, fashion, entertainment, and so on? Aren't we also the recipients of someone else's judgment? Most people have felt the self-righteous judgment of others, who imagine that they are superior to us and point out all of our flaws and mistakes.

The Lord Christ warned all of us not to judge in this way. He said,

> For with what judgment you judge, you will be judged; and with what measure you use, it will be measured back to you. And why do you look at the speck in your brother's eye, but do not consider the plank in your own eye? Or how can you say to your brother, let me remove the speck from your eye; and look a plank is in your own eye? First remove the plank

from your own eye, and then you will see clearly to remove the speck from your brother's eye. (Matthew 7:2–5)

Jesus also said in regard to judging, "Do not judge according to appearance, but judge with righteous judgment" (John 7:24). Here he reminds us to not judge in a superficial, self-righteousness, or legalistic way, rather, he wants us to go deeper in our observations and render sound judgments that are in harmony with the Word of God.

Confusion can set in when the popular concept of judging is imposed upon us. This kind of judgment argues that we're not supposed to judge anyone but to accept all just as they are without qualification. But this can't be true because there are things that are either right or wrong, true or false, and good or bad. There are also misguided people, false teachers who want others to follow them, and popular distortions of what is true and false.

Therefore, we're to fear God because he will bring us to judgment, including every secret thing in our lives, and judge us justly. God expects no less from us than we expect from him. It is a delusion to think that God does not know, does not see, or does not care about the things we do and say. God is just, and the coming judgment will be just. The Lord put it this way:

But I say to you that for every idle word that men may speak, they will give an account of it in the Day of Judgment. For by your words you will be justified and by your words you will be condemned. (Matthew 12:36–37)

This is an argument from the lesser to the greater. It implies that if God is so concerned with what we have to say, no matter how trivial it might seem to us, how much more will he condemn evil deeds?

John Macarthur comments on the severity Christ places on idle words: "The most seemingly insignificant sin—even a slip of the tongue—carries the full potential of all of hell's evil. No infraction against God's holiness is therefore a trifling thing, and each person will ultimately give account of every such indiscretion."[5]

Do you see why the popular mantra that "God is a god of love" is inadequate? Although it is true, it is inadequate because God is also just and holy and will hold all of us personally accountable for all we have ever done or said and all that we have failed to do or say.

Chapter 5

God Has Given All Judgment into the Hands of Christ

For the Father judges no one, but has committed all judgment to the Son, that all should honor the Son just as they honor the Father. He who does not honor the Son does not honor the Father who sent him. Most assuredly, I say to you, he who hears my word and believes in him who sent me, has everlasting life, and shall not come into judgment, but has passed from death into life. Most assuredly, I say to you, the hour is coming and now is, when the dead will hear the voice of the Son of God; and those who hear will live. For as the Father has life in himself, so he has granted the Son to have life in himself, and has given him authority to execute judgment, because he is the Son of Man. Do not marvel at this; for the hour is coming in which all who are in the graves will hear his voice and come forth—those who have done good, to the resurrection of life, and those who have done evil, to the resurrection of condemnation. I can of myself do nothing. As I hear, I judge; and my judgment is righteous, because I do not seek my own will but the will of the Father who sent me. (John 5:22–30)

WHY IS IT IMPORTANT TO KNOW THAT GOD THE Father has given Christ authority to judge all humans? It is because he is both fully man and fully God. This argument of necessity was made famous by Anselm of Canterbury (1033–1109).

> Anselm concludes that a God-Man was required to make payment for human sin. As previously mentioned, the payment for sin must be more valuable than all creation, and so could not be from the creation itself. If the payer of human debt must offer something "of his own" then this payer must be greater than all creation, i.e., God himself. However, this one also must be human, since "none but true man owes" the debt of human sin. Hence, the need for the God-Man—Christ. Anselm describes how Christ's sacrifice was a proper and sufficient payment for human sin. He argues that "laying down his life, or giving himself up to death", was a proper payment, since the thing offered by the God-Man "must be found in himself," (nothing outside of God could make adequate payment), and since the God-Man, as God, is sinless and therefore not obliged to die as sinful humans are. Moreover, the payment was made to God in so far as it was offered in the cause of justice. The implied premise is that all justice honors God. The payment was sufficiently large since a sin against the person of Christ, the God-Man, is infinitely worse than all other sins, suggesting that Christ's life must be an equal but oppositely infinite loveable good. The offering of such a life thus more than pays the human debt. In light of Christ's nonobligatory offering for human sin, God owed him a reward of equal value. Since—as God—Christ needed nothing, he assigned "the fruit and recompense of his death" to those he came to redeem, human beings.[6]

Therefore, as the Son of God, Christ can save those who believe. As the Son of man, Christ can and will execute judgment on all humans. The apostle Paul made this clear in the book of Acts.

Truly, these times of ignorance God overlooked, but now commands all men everywhere to repent, because he has appointed a day on which he will judge the world in righteousness by the Man He has ordained (Jesus Christ). He has given assurance of this to all by raising him from the dead. (Acts 17:30–31)

We know that it is impossible for God to lie (see Hebrews 6:18), so when he said, "He has appointed a day on which he will judge the world in righteousness by the Man He has ordained (Jesus Christ)," we can be fully confident that it will happen. Judgment Day has been scheduled. It has been foreordained and predestined by God to take place, and all history is moving in that direction.

> We must all stand before the judgment seat of Christ. For it is written: As I live says the Lord, every knee shall bow to me, and every tongue confess to God. So then each of us shall give account of himself to God. (Romans 14:10–12)

What is it that we shall all, without exception, confess to God? We shall all confess to God that Jesus Christ is Lord. The apostle Paul wrote,

> Let this mind be in you which was also in Christ Jesus, who being in the form of God, did not consider it robbery to be equal with God, but made himself of no reputation, taking the form of a bond servant, and coming in the likeness of men. And being found in appearance as a man, he humbled himself and became obedient to the point of death, even the death of the cross. Therefore God also has highly exalted him, and given him the name which is above every name, that at the name of Jesus every knee should bow, of those in heaven, and of those on earth, and of those under the earth,

and that every tongue should confess that Jesus Christ is Lord, to the glory of God the Father. (Philippians 2:5–11)

This day has been scheduled by God. All of human history is inexorably moving to this day, which has been appointed by God. No one and nothing can stop it. Every person who has ever lived will be there and will first make the confession that Jesus Christ is Lord, either voluntarily or by compulsion. Either way, this confession will be made. Then everyone will give an account to God.

Judgment Day will be the day when God renders life or death, each according to his or her deeds.

God will render to each one according to his deeds, eternal life to those who by patient continuance in doing good, seek for glory, honor, and immortality; but to those who are self-seeking and do not obey the truth, but obey unrighteousness—indignation and wrath, tribulation and anguish, on every soul of man who does evil. (Romans 2:6–9)

We're also told that on Judgment Day, God will judge the secrets of men by Jesus Christ according to the message given to Paul the apostle by God. The secrets of men include two things:

1. Hiding the evil we've done from public knowledge so that it is concealed to protect ourselves from the consequences of our actions
2. Hiding the motives behind our actions

Our motives are what drive us to do something or act in a certain way. We can hide our motives from other people but not from God. We're warned that the Word of God discovers our condition.

> For the Word of God is living and powerful, and sharper than any two-edged sword, piercing even to the division of soul and spirit, and of joints and marrow, and is a discerner of the thoughts and intents of the heart. And there is no creature hidden from his sight, but all things are naked and open to the eyes of him (Jesus Christ) to whom we must give account. (Hebrews 4:12–13)

Does this sound as if we can hide from God? Does this sound as if we can cover anything up from God? No! We can hide from others but not from God.

I once worked with a man who referred to something as "slower than the second coming of Christ." He said this for shock value and to show that he was a clever and interesting person, but it just sailed over the heads of those who heard him. If anything, they probably wondered, *What does this have to do with anything that we've been talking about?* I'm sure there were some who heard this and had no idea that Christ was supposed to come again a second time.

From a temporal perspective, the Second Coming of Christ and Judgment Day do seem overly delayed but not from an eternal perspective. Both have been scheduled on the divine calendar and will take place. In fact, God's delay works to our advantage, giving us time to repent. We are not to mock God by saying he is slow or that he will not judge us. We shouldn't act as if this will never happen or that we don't really believe, but rather, we should dread them both. Listen to the warnings of the prophets Amos and Zephaniah.

> Woe to you who desire the Day of the Lord! For what good is the Day of the Lord to you? It will be darkness, and not light. It will be as though a man fled from a lion, and a bear met him! Or as though he went into the house, leaned his hand on the wall, and a serpent bit him! Is not the Day of

the Lord darkness, and not light? Is it not very dark, with no brightness in it? (Amos 5:18–20)

The great day of the Lord is near; it is near and hastens quickly. The noise of the day of the Lord is bitter; there the mighty men shall cry out. That day is the day of wrath, a day of trouble and distress, a day of devastation and desolation, a day of darkness and gloominess, a day of clouds and thick darkness, a day of trumpet and alarm against the fortified cities, and against the high towers. (Zephaniah 1:14–16)

Before this happens and the world approaches these worsening conditions, many will mistakenly hope for the Day of the Lord thinking it will bring relief, but it will only bring the judgment of God upon the world. Therefore, we should not scoff at the slowness of its coming but rather be thankful for the delay. Neither should we entertain false hopes about the Day of the Lord, for it brings judgment that will engulf the whole earth.

CHAPTER 6

What Are Christ's Qualifications to Judge Us?

CHRIST IS QUALIFIED TO JUDGE THE WORLD BECAUSE he is the creator of it.

> He (Jesus Christ) is the image of the invisible God, the firstborn over all creation. For by him all things were created that are in heaven and that are on earth, visible and invisible, whether thrones or dominions or principalities or powers. All things were created through him (Jesus Christ) and for him. And he is before all things, and in him all things consist (hold together). And he is the head of the body, the church, who is the beginning, the firstborn from the dead, that in all things he might have the preeminence. (Colossians 1:15–18)

His number one qualification to judge the people on earth is that he is the creator of all things. This is clearly seen in the passage above. He is the creator of all things, and they were made by him, through him, and for him.

Christ was framed as the creator to establish his divinity, which has been perennially under assault down through the ages. Why should men believe that Christ was the Creator? I have already argued that we must believe the way God has presented himself. He has also presented Christ as such. We must not reject it because it isn't what we prefer or what we want to believe about him.

The apostle John, who was a disciple of Christ, wrote this about Jesus: "In the beginning was the Word, and the Word was with God, and the Word was God. He was in the beginning with God. All things were made through him, and without him nothing was made that was made" (John 1:1–3). It was written this way to highlight Christ's divinity and eternality as the cocreator of all things.

Another passage supports Christ as the creator of all things.

> God who at various times and in various ways spoke in time past to the fathers by the prophets, has in these last days spoken to us by his Son, whom he has appointed heir of all things, through whom he also made the worlds; who being the brightness of his glory and the express image of his person, and upholding all things by the word of his power, when he had by himself purged our sins, sat down at the right hand of the majesty on high, having become so much better than the angels, as he has by inheritance obtained a more excellent name than they. (Hebrews 1:1–4)

Again, why is the Lord qualified to be our judge? It is because he is our creator. In the account of creation, the Lord made man from the dust of the earth and breathed into his nostrils the breath of life. Man became a living being (see Genesis 2:7). From this one man, Adam, came all people, thus all people belong to the Lord and are responsible to God, owing him glory and honor for their creation. Christ was our creator and as a result, has become our judge, to whom we are responsible.

God who made the world and everything in it, since he is Lord of heaven and earth, does not dwell in temples made by hands. Nor is he worshipped with men's hands, as though he needed anything, since he gives to all life, breath, and all things. And he has made from one blood every nation of men to dwell on all the face of the earth, and has determined their pre-appointed times, and the boundaries of their dwellings, so that they should seek the Lord, in the hope that they might grope for him and find him, though he is not far from each of us. (Acts 17:24–27)

Here we see again the Lord as our creator, having made all people through one man. The Apostle Paul presented this argument to the Athenian philosophers who worshipped many gods and idols and even one to the "unknown god" (Acts 17:23). This unknown god, Paul said, "I proclaim to you" (Acts 17:24). This unknown god, whom they worshipped but did not know, was the Creator. This God, whom they did not know, was the one who determined the destinies of individuals and nations, regulated the span of their lives and the ruling times of their nations, and created circumstances that would prompt them to seek after him. This god, whom they did not know, was destined to be their judge—a worthy one as their creator.

Job, in the Old Testament, records the Lord's words to him in a final rebuke: "Everything under heaven is mine" (Job 41:11). In other words, the Lord owes nothing to anyone nor does he need to buy anything that he would have to repay. The Lord is completely sovereign, and everything under heaven is his. Likewise, the psalms affirm the same thing. "The heavens are yours, the earth is also yours; the world and all its fullness you have founded them. The north and the south, you have created them" (Psalm 89:10–11).

All such biblical affirmations of these truths are meant to disarm our excuses and instill fear of the Lord, who is and who will be our judge. Because all things belong to him and he owes no one anything, he bows to no one, unlike some judges in our world who cave under peer pressure, social pressure, political pressure, special interest groups, and lobbyists. The Lord remains sovereign and almighty above all, implementing righteousness and justice in accord with his nature.

Christ is also qualified to judge us because he knows the human heart. "Therefore judge nothing before the time, until the Lord comes, who will both bring to light the hidden things of darkness and reveal the counsels of the heart" (1 Corinthians 4:5). This refers to the thoughts and inner motives of man, something only the Lord can know and judge accurately.

Isn't it a little unnerving to hear that the Lord knows the counsels of our hearts? In other words, he knows us better than we know ourselves. He knows our inner deliberations, debates, insecurities, fears, drives, ambitions, and plans. All the while, we think that the counsels of our own hearts are safe, secure, hidden from all, and something that no one has access to. By such knowledge, the Lord is in no way intruding into our lives. It is just that God cannot *not* be God, therefore, all things are opened and laid bare before him. This should strike fear in the hearts of all who are relying on outward service but not on inner devotion, for without both we will suffer loss.

It also seems remarkable to me that people can experience profound suffering through war, crime, disease, and poor decision-making, on our part or on behalf of others, on a daily basis throughout the world but dismiss a future judgment by God as improbable, even though we render judgment and condemnation and punish all such evil. But just as there are real and deadly consequences for our decisions in this life, so there will be real and eternal consequences in the life to come.

Again, here is the admonition of Solomon: "Fear God and keep his commandments, for this is man's all. For God will bring every work into judgment, including every secret thing, whether good or evil" (Ecclesiastes 12:13–14).

CHAPTER 7

When Will the Judgment Day Take Place?

And as it is appointed for men to die once, but after this the judgment. (Hebrews 9:27)

THIS IS WHAT WE KNOW ABOUT IT: JUST AS WE KNOW we all will die and have an appointment with death that nothing can stop, so we have an appointment to be judged by Christ. One follows the other! Right now, our only frame of reference is this world. We understand the concept of an appointment, the slow demise of our bodies, and our eventual deaths, but a future day after our deaths where God judges us is too abstract for our minds to understand and requires that we embrace God's disclosure of it in scripture.

Thankfully, we still have funerals and obituaries, but even these reminders of death are so sanitized that the impact of death is minimized. In the town where I live, a local cemetery advertises, "How do you want to be remembered?" They know that the time of death is confusing and that preplanning can help us organize our thoughts and spare others the burden of doing it.

The problem, of course, is that we see ourselves differently than others see us. So, which is more accurate, how we see ourselves or how others see us? If it is left to us, we will probably put our best foot forward in our own eulogy and leave out our flaws and other failures. If our family and friends do our eulogy, they will probably do the same. We see this regularly in the obituaries of the local newspaper. There we read about some of the deceased's accomplishments. We also read about how that person loved sports, had a good sense of humor, adored all the nieces and nephews, and left behind a spouse and children.

It is appropriate that when a fellow creature dies, we should honor that person as best we can without denigrating his or her memory. What concerns me today is the trend where there is no funeral but a celebration of life gathering. Frequently, the deceased requests this before dying. At these celebrations, there is no mention of God, except in a generic way, but only a simple commiseration over the death of the deceased, as people hope that sharing fond memories of the person will induce God to admit that person into heaven. This is unlikely. If God wasn't honored in the deceased's life or death, then there probably wasn't any faith in God in the first place.

Here we come, face-to-face again, with the issue of what a person wants to believe about God versus how God has presented himself to us. What we want to believe about God is irrelevant unless it harmonizes with the biblical declaration. The biblical declaration that I'm working with at the moment is, "It is appointed for men to die once, but after this the judgment" (Hebrews 9:27). This may not be appropriate at most funerals, but it certainly needs to be proclaimed in churches and other venues to forewarn those who are in denial.

Who is in denial? Three types of people are in denial. The first are nonreligious people who wonder if there isn't more to life than what meets the eye. Then there are apostates, who once embraced the Gospel of Christ but afterward rejected and walked away from it. The third are adversaries of the Gospel of Christ, who actively form opposition to God and his plan of salvation.

All of these will experience "a certain fearful expectation of judgment, and fiery indignation which will devour the adversaries" (Hebrews 10:27). This will happen as they near death and their consciences bring to mind what they have done and condemn them for it.

There are actually two judgment days.

The first judgment will be for the Christian: "For we must all appear before the judgment seat of Christ, that each one may receive the things done in the body, according to what we have done, whether good or bad" (2 Corinthians 5:10).

John Macarthur comments on this and writes,

> The judgment seat of Christ metaphorically refers to the place where the Lord will sit to evaluate the believers' lives for the purpose of giving them eternal rewards. It is translated from the Greek word "bema", which was an elevated platform where victorious athletes (e.g. during the Olympics) went to receive their crowns. The term is also used to the place of judging as when Jesus stood before Pontius Pilate. But here the reference is definitely the athletic analogy. Corinth had such a platform where both athletic rewards and legal justice were dispensed, so the Corinthians understood Paul's reference. The things done in the body refer to actions which happened during the believer's time of ministry. This does not include sins, since their judgment took place at the cross (of Christ). Paul was referring to all of those activities believers do during their lifetimes, which relate to their eternal reward and praise from God. What Christians do with their temporal bodies will, in God's eyes have an eternal impact.[7]

While this is an award ceremony, it will still hold potential loss or great reward but does not refer to judgment for sins since Christ bore them for us. Our salvation is eternally secure.

The second day of judgment is for the unrepentant sinner.

> Then I saw a great white throne and him who sat on it, from whose face the earth and the heaven fled away. And there was found no place for them. And I saw the dead, small and great standing before God, and books were opened. And another book was opened, which is the Book of Life. And the dead were judged according to their works, by the things which were written in the books. The sea gave up the dead who were in it, and Death and Hades delivered up the dead who were in them. And they were judged, each one according to his works. Then death and Hades were cast into the lake of fire. This is the second death. And anyone not found in the Book of life was cast into the lake of fire. (Revelation 20:11–15)

This is the final picture of human history as we currently know it. Here we see Christ seated on the white throne of judgment. Remember, God the Father has committed all judgment to Christ (see John 5:27), as both Son of God and Son of man. This mass of humanity will bow to Christ (see Philippians 2:9–11), as they now see him as Lord and Judge seated on the great white throne, symbolizing his purity and holiness.

This courtroom scene is a one of judgment, condemnation, and sentencing. There is no advocate for the prosecution or for the defense. Instead, there are only books of evidence proving their guilt before God. Everything a person has done, thought, or said has been recorded and reviewed by God. This will culminate in all people standing before Christ to receive their sentences. This is why we're to fear God!

Don't we currently experience real consequences for the things we do and don't do—even the consequence of physical death? Isn't this world full of misery and suffering? Then why would someone think it strange that a more perfect judgment awaits us? Doesn't this logic cohere? Isn't the judgment of God connected naturally and logically from this world to the coming world?

I believe that the various forms of judgments and consequences we experience now *are* naturally and logically connected to the future judgment and condemnation of God. Therefore, we should fear God because the "second death" is a death that does not end. Augustine put it this way:

> Nevertheless with the help of the grace of our Redeemer we may be enabled to decline (or avoid) that second death. For that death, which means not the separation of the soul from the body but the union of both for eternal punishment, is a more grievous death; it is the worst of all evils. There, by contrast, men will not be in the situations of "before death' and "after death", but always "in death", and for this reason they will never be living, never dead, but dying for all eternity. In fact, man will never be "in death" in a more horrible sense than in that state where death itself will be deathless.[8]

Remember Solomon's conclusion about our lives: "Let us hear the conclusion of the whole matter: Fear God and keep his commandments, for this is man's all. For God will bring every work into judgment. Including every secret thing, whether good or evil" (Ecclesiastes 12:13–14).

PART 2

Three Past Examples of Judgment that Affirm the Future Day of God's Judgment

ALL THREE EXAMPLES ARE GIVEN AS PROOF OF GOD'S
eventual judgment on those who live ungodly lives.

> For if God did not spare the angels who sinned, but cast
> them down to hell and delivered them into chains of
> darkness, to be reserved for judgment; and did not spare
> the ancient world, but saved Noah, one of eight people,
> a preacher of righteousness, bringing in the flood on the
> world of the ungodly; and turning the cities of Sodom and
> Gomorrah into ashes, condemned them to destruction,
> making them an example to those who afterward would
> live ungodly. (2 Peter 2:4–6)

John Macarthur comments on this passage and writes:

> Lest anyone think that God is too loving and merciful to
> judge the wicked false teachers and their deceived people,

Peter gives three powerful illustrations of past divine judgment on the wicked. Though God has no pleasure in the death of the wicked (Ezekiel 33:11) God must judge wickedness because his holiness requires it.[9]

CHAPTER 8

The First Example: Angels Who Sinned

PETER'S FIRST EXAMPLE HAS TO DO WITH THE ANGELS who sinned. God did not spare these angels but cast them down to hell and delivered them into chains of darkness [imprisonment], to be reserved for judgment. This example is found in Jude 6 and Genesis 6:1–3. The angels had crossed a boundary that God had set for them when they had sexual relations with women.

Just as God has set boundaries for angels, so he has set boundaries for men.

> God, who made the world and everything in it, since he is Lord of heaven and earth, does not dwell in temples made with hands. Nor is he worshiped with men's hands, as though he needed anything, since he gives to all life and breath, and all things. And he has made from one blood every nation of men to dwell on all the face of the earth, and has determined their pre-appointed times and the boundaries of their dwellings, so that they should seek the Lord, in the hope that they might grope for him and find him, though he is not far from each one of us. (Acts 17:24–27)

Again, notice how God is presented to us. There is no apology, no defense, no explanation, and no proof. He is seen here as highly exalted and independent of the created order and does not need our stamp of approval. My point is to show that not only is God the creator of all things but is also so involved in his creation that he has pre-appointed the time in which we live and the geographical boundaries of where we live.

Likewise, he has done the same for the angels, both the good and the bad ones. Their lives, like ours, are circumscribed by the sovereignty of God. When the angels sinned, boundaries were set for them, putting limits on what they could and couldn't do, especially to people, who were weaker than they were. So when they crossed that boundary, God cast them down to hell, bound and in darkness.

This particular place in hell is so dreadful that demons (fallen angels) plead not to be sent there. We see this in the account where Christ cast out a large number of demons from two possessed men.

> When he (Jesus) had come to the other side, to the country of the Gergesenes, there met him two demon-possessed men, coming out of the tombs, exceedingly fierce, so that no one could pass that way. And suddenly they cried out, saying, what have we to do with you, Jesus, you Son of God? Have you come here to torment us before the time [Day of Judgment]? Now a good way off from them there was a heard of many swine feeding. So the demons begged him, saying, if you cast us out, permit us to go away into the herd of swine. And he (Jesus) said to them, go. So when they had come out, they went into the herd of swine. And suddenly the whole herd of swine ran violently down the steep place into the sea, and perished in the water. (Matthew 8:28–32, Luke 8:31)

Their pleading to not be sent to this abyss, where the demons from long ago had been bound in this underworld prison, indicated their eternal torment had already begun. This summary of hell is a good corrective for the foolish cartoonist who oftentimes portrays it as a place where the demons are like prison guards poking the human population with their pitchforks. This is not so! Instead, it is described as "a place of outer darkness where there will be weeping and gnashing of teeth" (Matthew 8:12). John Macarthur comments on this and says, "This speaks of inconsolable grief and unremitting torment."[10]

While these accounts of evil and fallen angels may seem cryptic to us—that is, mysterious and baffling—they are no more so than the world in which we live. As the morning light began to illuminate your bedroom, did it dawn on you when you woke up this morning, looked down at your dog at the foot of the bed, and glanced at your wife, who was rolled up in her blankets like a mummy, that over the last eight hours, the earth rotated at one thousand miles per hour, and you orbited in space around the sun at sixty-seven thousand miles per hour? At the same time, our entire solar system traveled 515,000 miles per hour through the Milky Way galaxy.

Then you put on your robe and one slipper, because the other one was under the bed and too hard to reach, and walked outside into the front yard to pick up the newspaper from the wet grass. As you walked back to the house, you were grateful that at least one foot was dry. You then turned on the television for the local news to find that there had been a traffic accident and that movement had been reduced to stop and go. Isn't it amazing that billions of solar systems are traveling at hundreds of thousands of miles per hour without ever coming to a standstill?

Which seems stranger: a universe where there is an almighty

God who punished wicked angels for crossing a forbidden boundary, incarcerated them until a day of judgment, and used their destiny to warn us that we, too, would face a judgment day, or a universe that spins, revolves, and rotates at tremendous speeds in a crowded universe? I find them to both be baffling but equally compelling and true.

The prison for fallen angels as imagined by painter
John Martin called "Pandemonium".

CHAPTER 9

The Second Example: The Worldwide Flood

THE SECOND PAST EXAMPLE OF JUDGMENT IS FROM the worldwide flood. Just as hell has been mocked by cartoonists, who try to diminish the biblical account through humor, so the biblical account of the worldwide flood has been reduced to a warm story of God saving animals. Children's books, wall hangings, and paintings have often changed the narrative from God's judgment on humankind to a rescue operation by God to save animals. My wife and I had such a painting hanging on our wall. The picture was of a large boat rocking back and forth on a wave-tossed sea with animals snug and secure inside, peering out the open widows.

While this introduction to the great human tragedy is probably age appropriate for young children, it is equally appropriate for adults to think soberly about God's judgment of humankind, at this particular time, and not to imagine that this story of the flood is mere allegory of God's love for animals. An allegory is a story in which people, things, and happenings have a hidden or symbolic meaning and is often used to explain ideas and/or moral principles. An allegory has an appropriate place when looking at difficult or disturbing realities and makes them less shocking to human psychology.

However, the biblical story of the worldwide flood is not an allegory, which tries to convey a hidden or symbolic meaning. We know this because of the large amount of detail that is repeated over and over. It is rather the historical account of God's judgment on all humankind.[11] For those of you who have succumbed to the belief that the worldwide flood is allegory or mythology or have never read the account, I plan on quoting extensively from its account in Genesis 5–8 to show that there is no hidden or symbolic meaning but rather a clear historical account of God's judgment.

> This is the book of the genealogy of Adam. In the day that God created man, he made him in the likeness of God. He created them male and female and blessed them and called them mankind in the day they were created. And Adam lived one hundred and thirty years, and begot a son in his own likeness, and after his image, and named him Seth. After he begot Seth, the days of Adam were eight hundred years; and he had sons and daughters. So all the days that Adam lived were nine hundred and thirty years; and he died. (Genesis 5:1–5)

There are two purposes for this account of Adam's genealogy. The first is to show that humans lived long lives. The second is that there would have been large populations of people throughout the world, at that time, due to long their lives and a good environment.

I will now give a summary of Adam's partial genealogy. It is partial because although it mentions other sons and daughters, it only accounts for those who will move us toward Noah: Enosh lived 905 years, Cainan lived 910 years, Mahalalel lived 895 years, Jared lived 962 years, Enoch lived 365 years, Methuselah lived 969 years, and Lamech lived 182 years and his son was Noah. Then Lamech lived until he was 777 years and then died (see Genesis 5:4–31).

Therefore, I assume that because of long life spans and a good environment, there were large populations of people on the earth as the day of their judgment drew near, compounding the tragedy and devastation. This also corresponds to the need for a worldwide flood, since all humankind had become so thoroughly corrupt.

> Now it came to pass, when men began to multiply on the face of the earth, and daughters were born to them, that the sons of God (fallen angels) saw the daughters of men, that they were beautiful; and they took wives for themselves of all whom they chose.
>
> And the Lord said my spirit shall not strive with man forever, for he is indeed flesh yet his days shall be 120 years [the time remaining before the flood]. There were giants on the earth in those days And the Lord said, my Spirit shall not strive with man forever, for he is indeed flesh, yet his days and also afterward, when the sons of God came in to the daughters of men and they bore children to them. These were the mighty men who were of old, men of renown.
>
> Then the Lord saw that the wickedness of man was great in the earth, and that every intent of the thoughts of his heart was only evil continually [This was God's indictment against man and the reason for the flood]. And the Lord was sorry he had made man on the earth, and he was grieved in his heart. So the Lord said, I will destroy man whom I have created from the face of the earth, both man and beast, creeping things and the birds of the air, for I am sorry that I have made them. But Noah found grace in the eyes of the Lord.

This is the genealogy of Noah. Noah was a just man, perfect in his generations. Noah walked with God. And Noah begot three sons: Shem, Ham and Japheth. The earth also was corrupt before God, and the earth was filled with violence. So God looked upon the earth, and indeed it was corrupt, for all flesh had corrupted their way on the earth.

And God said to Noah, the end of all flesh has come before me, for the earth is filled with violence through them; and behold, I will destroy them with the earth. Make yourself an Ark of gopher wood; make rooms in the ark, and cover it inside and out with pitch. And this is how you shall make it: The length of the Ark shall be 300 cubits, its width 50 cubits, and its height 30 cubits. You shall make a window for the ark, and shall finish it to a cubit from above; and set the door of the ark in its side. You shall make it with a lower, second, and third decks. And behold, I myself am bringing floodwaters on the earth, to destroy from under heaven all flesh in which is the breath of life; everything that is on the earth shall die. But I will establish my covenant with you; and you shall go into the ark—you, your sons, your wife, and your sons' wives with you. And of every living thing of all flesh you shall bring two of every sort into the ark, to keep them alive with you; they shall be male and female. Of the birds after their kind, of animals after their kind, and of every creeping thing of the earth after its kind, two of every kind will come to you to keep them alive. And you shall take of all food that is eaten, and you shall gather it to yourself; and it shall be food for you and for them. Thus Noah did; according to all that God had commanded him, so he did. (Genesis 6)

While this account is picked apart because of its supposedly faulty science, poor geology, and unbelievable floodwaters reaching the tops of the mountains, there are reasonable explanations for all these things. However, that isn't my goal in presenting the story of Noah. My goal is to show that the worldwide flood was God's judgment on humankind.

> Then the Lord said to Noah, come into the ark, you and all your household, because I have seen that you are righteous before me in this generation. You shall take with you seven each of every clean animal, a male and female; two each of animals that are unclean, a male and a female; also seven each of birds of the air, male and female, to keep the species alive on the face of all the earth. For after seven more days I will cause it to rain on the earth forty days and forty nights, and I will destroy from the face of the earth all living things that I have made. And Noah did according to all that the Lord commanded him. Noah was 600 years old when the flood waters were on the earth.

> So Noah, with his sons, his wife, and his sons' wives, went into the ark because of the waters of the flood. Of clean animals, of animals that are unclean, of birds, and of everything that creeps on the earth, two by two they went into the ark to Noah, male and female, as God had commanded Noah. And it came to pass after seven days that the waters of the flood were on the earth. In the sixth hundredth year of Noah's life, in the second month, the seventeenth day of the month, on that day all the fountains of the great deep were broken up, and the windows of heaven were opened. And the rain was on the earth forty days and forty nights.

> On the very same day Noah and Noah's sons, Shem Ham, and Japheth, and Noah' wife and the three wives of his sons with them, entered the ark—they and every beast after its kind, all cattle after their kind, every creeping

thing that creeps on the earth after its kind, and every bird after its kind, every bird of every sort. And they went into the ark to Noah, two by two, of all flesh in which is the breath of life. So those that entered, male and female of all flesh went in as God had commanded him; and the Lord shut him in.

Now the flood was on the earth forty days. The waters increased and lifted up the ark, and it rose high above the earth. The waters prevailed and greatly increased on the earth, and the ark moved about on the surface of the waters. And the waters prevailed exceedingly on the earth, and all the high hills under the whole heaven were covered. The waters prevailed fifteen cubits upward, and the mountains were covered. And all flesh died that moved on the earth: birds, and cattle and beasts and every creeping thing that creeps on the earth, and every man. All in whose nostrils was the breath of the spirit of life, all that was on dry land, died. So he destroyed all living things which were on the face of the ground: both man and cattle, creeping thing and bird of the air. They were destroyed from the earth. Only Noah and those who were with him in the ark remained alive. And the waters prevailed on the earth one hundred and fifty days.

Then God remembered Noah, and every living thing, and all the animals that were with him in the ark. And God made a wind to pass over the earth, and the water subsided. The fountains of the deep and the windows of heaven were also stopped, and the rain from heaven was restrained. And the waters receded continually from the earth. At the end of the hundred and fifty days Then God remembered Noah, and every living thing, and all the animals that were with him in the ark. And God made a wind to pass over the earth, and the waters subsided. The fountains of the deep and the waters decreased. Then the ark rested in the seventh month, the seventeenth day of the month, on the mountains of Ararat. And the waters decreased continually until the tenth month. In the tenth month, on the first day of the month, the tops of the mountains were seen.

So it came to pass, at the end of forty days, that Noah opened the window of the ark which he had made. Then he sent out a raven, which kept going to and fro until the waters had dried up from the earth. He also sent out from himself a dove, to see if the waters had receded from the face of the ground. But the dove found no resting place for the sole of her foot, and she returned into the ark to him, for the waters were on the face of the whole earth. So he put out his hand and took her, and drew her into the ark to himself. And he waited yet another seven days and again he sent out the dove out from the ark. Then the dove came to him in the evening, and behold, a freshly plucked olive leaf was in her mouth; and Noah knew that the waters had receded from the earth. So he waited another seven days and sent out the dove, which did not return to him anymore.

And it came to pass in the sixth hundred and first year, in the first month, the first day of the month that the waters were dried up from the earth; and Noah removed the covering of the ark and looked, and indeed the surface of the ground was dry. And in the second month, on the twenty-seventh day of the month, the earth was dried.

Then God spoke to Noah, saying, go out of the ark, you and your wife, and your sons and your sons' wives with you. Bring out with you every living thing of all flesh that is with you: birds and cattle, and every creeping thing that creeps on the earth, so that they may abound on the earth, and be fruitful and multiply on the earth. So

Noah went out, and his sons and his wife, and his sons wives with him. Every animal, every creeping thing, every bird, and whatever creeps on the earth, according to their families, went out of the ark. (Genesis 7, 8:1–19)

Again, in my opinion, this is not the language of allegory. From the *Encyclopedia of the Bible* we read, "Allegory literally means to speak in a way that is other than what is meant."[12] Instead, the account of Noah is closer to a travelogue with dates, times, and repetition of details, which lends itself more to a historical account.

My last argument for the historicity of the flood comes from the Lord Christ Jesus himself. He said in regards to his second coming,

But of that day and hour no one knows, not even the angels of heaven, but my Father only. But as the days of Noah were, so also will the coming of the Son of Man be. For as in the days before the flood, they were eating and drinking, marrying and giving in marriage, until the day that Noah entered the ark, and did not know until the flood came and took them all away, so also will the coming of the Son of Man be. Then two men will be in the field: one will be taken the other one left. Two women will be grinding at the mill: one will be taken and the other left. Watch therefore, for you do not know what hour your Lord is coming. But know this, if the master of the house had known what hour the thief would come, he would have watched and not allowed his house to be broken into. Therefore you also be ready, for the Son of Man is coming at an hour you do not expect. (Matthew 24:36–44)

John Macarthur comments on this and writes,

Jesus' emphasis here is not is much the extreme wickedness of Noah's day, but on the people's preoccupation with mundane matters of everyday life (eating, drinking, marrying, and giving in marriage) when judgment fell suddenly. They had received warnings, in the form of Noah's preaching, and the ark itself, which was a testimony of the judgment to come. But they were unconcerned about such matters and therefore they were swept away unexpectedly in the midst of their daily activities.[13]

The Lord assumed the historical reality of Noah, God's condemnation of humankind at that time, the judgment of a worldwide flood that followed, and the saving of Noah and his family.

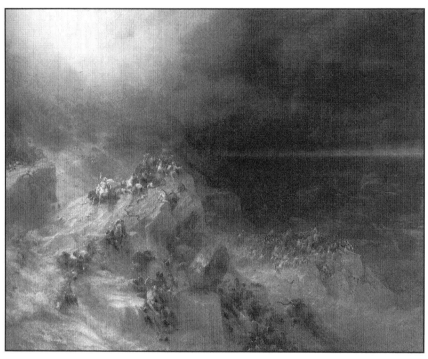

Noah's worldwide flood titled "The Great Deluge" by Ivan Alvazovsky.

CHAPTER 10

The Third Example: Sodom and Gomorrah

SODOM AND GOMORRAH ARE EXAMPLES OF SIN that has reached the point of no return. We saw it in the judgment of the fallen angels when they crossed the boundary God had set for them by having sexual relations with women (see Genesis 6:2 and 2 Peter 2:4). They were cast down to the deepest pit in hell, were bound, and are awaiting their future judgment and condemnation.

Likewise, the pre-flood world of long ago was totally corrupted by sin, so much so, that the thoughts of the people's hearts were of evil continually and the earth was filled with violence. They, too, reached the point of no return in their corruption, and God's judgment swept them away in a worldwide flood.

Our final example of God's judgment is his destruction of the cities of Sodom and Gomorrah. This story is nuanced differently from the other two stories in that "a great outcry" came to God's attention because their sin [The people of Sodom and Gomorrah] "was very grave" (Genesis 18:20).

Where did the great outcry come from? We don't know. Perhaps it came from the victims of the "grave evil" in these two cities or maybe from the prayers of Abraham for his nephew Lot, who lived in Sodom. He had petitioned the Lord to spare the city of Sodom. The Lord had agreed as long as ten righteous people could be found there, but ten couldn't be found in Sodom so the judgment proceeded. This account is found in Genesis 19:1–29.

> Now the two angels [whom God sent to verify the outcry against the cities] came to Sodom in the evening, and Lot was sitting in the gate of Sodom. When Lot saw them, he rose to meet them, and he bowed himself with his face to the ground. And he said, here now my lords, please turn in to your servant's house and spend the night, and wash your feet; then you may rise early and go on your way.
>
> And they said, no we will spend the night in the open square. But he insisted strongly; so they turned into him and entered his house. Then he made them a feast, and baked unleavened bread, and they ate.
>
> Now before they lay down, the men of the city, the men of Sodom, both old and young, all the people from every quarter, surrounded the house. And they called to Lot and said to him, where are the men who came to you tonight? Bring them out to us that we may know them carnally [sexually).
>
> So Lot went out to them through the doorway, shut the door behind him, and said, please, my brethren, do not do so wickedly! See now, I have two daughters who have not known a man, please, let me bring them out to you, and you may do to them as you wish; [Lot's reasoning and judgment were compromised from living under Sodom's evil influence] only do nothing to these men, since this is the reason they have come under the shadow of my roof.

And they said stand back. Then they said this one came in to stay here, and he keeps acting as a judge; now we will deal worse with you than with them. So they pressed hard against the man Lot, and came near to break down the door. But the men [Lot's guests who were really angels from God] reached out their hands and pulled Lot into the house with them, and shut the door. And they struck the men who were at the doorway of the house with blindness, both small and great, so that they became weary trying to find the door.

Then the men said to Lot, have you anyone else here? Son-in-law, your sons, your daughters, and whomever you have in the city—take them out of this place! For we will destroy this place, because the outcry against them has grown great before the face of the Lord, and the Lord has sent us to destroy it.

So Lot went out and spoke to his sons-in-law, who had married his daughters, and said, get up, get out of this place; for the Lord will destroy this city! But to his sons-in-law he seemed to be joking.

When the morning dawned, the angels urged Lot to hurry, saying, arise, take your wife, and your two daughters who are here, lest you be consumed in the city. And while he lingered, the men took hold of his hand, and his wife's hand, and the hands of his two daughters, the Lord being merciful to him, and brought him out and set him outside the city. So it came to pass, when they had brought him outside, that he said, escape for your life! Do not look behind you nor stay anywhere in the plain. Escape to the mountains, lest you be destroyed.

Then Lot said to them, please, no, my lords! Indeed now, your servant has found favor in your sight and you have increased your mercy which you have shown me by saving my life; but I cannot escape to the mountains, lest some evil overtake me and I die. See now this city is near enough to flee to, and it is a little one; please let me escape there (is it not a little one?) And my soul shall live.

And he said to him, see I have favored you concerning this thing also, in that I will not over- throw this city for which you have spoken. Hurry, escape there. For I cannot do anything until you arrive there. Therefore the name of the city was called Zoar.

The Sun had risen upon the earth when Lot entered Zoar. Then the Lord rained brimstone and fire on Sodom and Gomorrah, from the Lord out of the heavens. So he overthrew those cities, all the plain, all the inhabitants of the cities, and what grew on the ground.

But his wife looked back behind him, and she became a pillar of salt.

And Abraham went early in the morning to the place where he had stood before the Lord. Then he looked toward Sodom and Gomorrah, and toward all of the land of the plain, and he saw, and behold, the smoke of the land which went up like the smoke of a furnace. And it came to pass, when God destroyed the cites of the plain, that God remembered Abraham, and sent Lot out of the midst of the overthrow, when he overthrew the cities in which Lot had dwelt."

Sodom and Gomorrah have become catchwords for both evil and destruction by the hand of God. By this means, the names of Sodom and Gomorra have entered the human psyche, the fear of sudden and complete destruction by the hand of God, at least wherever the church is found which proclaims these judgments of God.

Many people dislike such a portrayal of God, believing that God is too nice to do such things. They believe this kind of behavior is beneath him and makes him look like a bully. Again, the question that is begging to be asked is, which statement is true: What I want to believe about God or how God has presented himself to us? I believe the latter is true.

In the account of Sodom and Gomorrah, the Lord appeared to Abraham in Genesis 18 and divulged the reason he planned to go to Sodom and Gomorrah. He told Abraham, "Because the outcry against Sodom and Gomorrah is great, and because their sin is very grave, I will go down now and see whether they have done altogether according to the outcry against it that has come me; and if not, I will know" (Genesis 18:21). [If so, he would destroy them.]

Take careful note of two things about the Lord. First, he doesn't delight in the death of the wicked. Their death and destruction are an absolute necessity to God because he is the moral governor of the universe (see Ezekiel 18:23). Second, he has the right, the will, and the determination to put them to death.

"The firestorm of God's wrath about to incinerate
Sodom and Gomorrah" by John Martin

CHAPTER 11

What We Are to Learn from These Examples

FIRST OF ALL, WE'RE TO LEARN THAT A PRECEDENT was set. A precedent is defined as, "An act, statement, legal decision, case, etc. that may serve as an example, reason, justification, for a later one."[14] God's judgment of the fallen angels, humankind being destroyed in the flood, and the incineration of the cities Sodom and Gomorrah, all serve as examples of God's judgment being rendered and his final judgment still pending for them.

Therefore, the ancient fallen angels, who have been imprisoned in the deepest depths of hell, violent, sinful humankind, which was destroyed by the flood, and the citizens of Sodom and Gomorrah, who were destroyed by fire, are likewise incarcerated in hell and are awaiting the final Day of Judgment by Christ.

These three examples of God's judgment serve as warnings to us. They warn us that God will hold all people personally accountable for all they have done and said. God can do this because he is omniscient. He knows all things, has a perfect memory, and documents everything—not even the intents of our hearts are hidden from him.

These three examples of God's judgment serve as warnings to us, whether we feel like a monster or not. Even the best of humanity, from our perspective, will be held accountable to God.

Do you remember Augustine's definition of evil? He said that evil didn't exist as a creation of God but rather, was the act of turning away from God, the eternal good, to look for satisfaction in the lesser goods that God had created. The awful irony of turning from God, who is the greatest good and alone can provide eternal happiness, is that it results in corruption, evil, misery, and unhappiness. Satan was the first to do this, then one third of heaven followed him and did it, and all of humankind has followed suit. The result is the corruption of our nature, which is responsible for all of the resulting evil in this world.

We've all missed the mark God set for us and for which we are accountable to God. As a result, unredeemed man will stand shoulder to shoulder with the fallen angels, pre-flood humanity, and the people of Sodom and Gomorrah at the great-white-throne judgment seat of Christ.

A precedent was set. These three examples of God's judgment assure us that the great and final judgment of God will take place—it is scheduled in the divine calendar—and its condemnation and destruction will be eternal.

Pheme Perkins asks a good question:

> Second Peter raises another question for Christians today. Are we too unconcerned about the truth of religious claims? Many people have accommodated the pluralism of our culture and even their own families by holding religious beliefs to be private and individual, not public. Parents whose young adult children no longer practice any identifiable form of Christianity often say to me, well, he (or she) really is a good kid, so it's okay with me. Of course, it's not quite okay or the person wouldn't have volunteered

that piece of information. College students make the same accommodation that their parents do when faced with the behavior on the part of a friend or roommate that makes them uncomfortable. "I really don't like his (or her) drinking, causal attitude towards sex; treatment of others; occasional drug use, or whatever, but otherwise they are okay. In other words, a general moral or behavioral test substitutes for belief, convictions, and in some cases even for a morally coherent way of life. Cultural attitudes like that are more effective and surreptitious false teachers than any group of persons within the church."[15]

This is the current moral track of many generations of people. That is, they hold religious beliefs to be private and individual (subjective) and not public or resembling anything biblical. They can, therefore, confer on themselves the freedom to believe whatever they want to believe about life or God.

But we have many warnings in scripture that tell us not to live ungodly lives. I used the examples of fallen angels crossing boundaries God had given to them, the destruction of pre-flood humankind for their incessant evil, and the destruction of Sodom and Gomorrah for their grave evil, but that's not all there is. The Old Testament is full of examples, warnings, and consequences for all who disobey God in willful and stubborn unbelief.

The New Testament gives us more warnings. We read in Galatians 5:19–21,

> Now the works of the flesh are evident, which are: adultery, fornication, uncleanness, lewdness, idolatry, sorcery, hatred, contentions, jealousies, outbursts of wrath, selfish ambitions, dissensions, heresies, envy, murders, drunkenness, revelries, and the like; of which I tell you beforehand, just as I also told you in time past, that those

who practice such things will not inherit the Kingdom
of God.

Take notice that these behaviors aren't personal, private, or
subjective. Rather, they are behaviors that God calls sinful and wrong
and expects them to be embraced universally as such. The continual
practice of such things—more examples can be found in Romans
1:24–32 and 1 Corinthians 6: 9–10—will keep you from inheriting
the kingdom of God. It doesn't matter if your religious beliefs are
private, personal, or subjective and allow you the freedom to excuse
yourself or others. If you practice such things, you will not enter the
kingdom of God. Rather, you will face the judgment of God, which
will confirm your condemnation.

PART 3

Let's Review

CHAPTER 12

Any Concept of God that Lacks His Judgment
of Men Is an Incomplete Picture of Him

AT THE BEGINNING OF THIS BOOK, I USED TWO illustrations where one person held to the belief that God was a god of love and celebration and the other held that God was a god of love and did not condemn. I wish I could have asked them both, how did you come up with that? Did you read it somewhere? Did God tell you that? Is this what you've discerned? Did you get it from your intuition? The problem is that all of this is subjective and therefore, in competition with about eight billion other opinions.

What we need is an ultimate reference point to be able to say God is love, and the only ultimate reference point is God. He has disclosed that he is indeed love.

> He who does not love does not know God, for God is love.
> (1 John 4:8)

But that disclosure is qualified, in that it is limited. John was not offering a definition of God. Listen to what A.W. Tozer says,

The Apostle John, by the Spirit, wrote, "God is love," and some have taken his words to be a definitive statement concerning the essential nature of God. This is a great error. John was by those words stating a fact, but he was not offering a definition.

Equating love with God is a major mistake which has produced much unsound religious philosophy and has brought forth a spate of vaporous poetry completely out of accord with the Holy Scriptures and altogether of another climate from that of historic Christianity.

Had the Apostle declared that love is what God is, we would be forced to infer that God is what love is. If literally God is love, then literally love is God, and we are all in duty bound to worship love as the only God there is. If love is equal to God then God is only equal to love, and God and love are identical. Thus we destroy the concept of personality in God and deny outright all his attributes save one, and that one we substitute for God. The God we have left is not the God of Israel; He is not the God and Father of our Lord Jesus Christ; He is not the God of the prophets and the Apostles; He is not the God of the saints and reformers and martyrs, nor yet the God of the theologians and hymnists of the church.

For our souls' sake we must learn to understand the scriptures. We must escape the slavery of words and give loyal adherence to meanings instead. Words should express ideas, not originate them. We say that God is love; we say that God is light; we say that Christ is truth; and we mean the words to be understood in much the same way that words are understood when we say of a man, "He is kindness itself." By so saying we are not stating that kindness and the man are identical, and no one understands our words in that sense.

The words; God is love, mean that love is an essential attribute of God. Love is something true of God but it is not God. It expresses the way God is in his unitary being, as do the words holiness, justice, faithfulness, and truth. Because God is immutable He always acts like himself, and because He is a unity He never suspends one of his attributes in order to exercise another.

From God's other known attributes we may learn much about his love. We can know, for instance, that because God is self-existent His love has no beginning; because He is eternal, His love can have no end; because He is infinite, it has no limit; because He is holy, it is the quintessence of all spotless purity; because he is immense, His love is an incomprehensively vast, bottomless shoreless sea before which we kneel in joyful silence and from which the loftiest eloquence retreats confused and abashed.[16]

Like Tozer said, "Love is something true about God but it is not God."[17] When people make the mistake of equating the two as one and the same, they are expressing what they want to believe about God but not what is true about God.

God warns us against this in the Old Testament book of Job. Job is forty-two chapters long. The opening chapter tells us of Job's devout life and a debate in heaven between Satan and the Lord. The Lord said to Satan,

"Have you considered my servant Job, that there is none like him on the earth, a blameless and upright man, one who fears God and shuns evil?" Satan replied: "Does Job fear God for nothing? Have you not built a hedge around him? Around his household, and around all that he has on every side? You have blessed the work of his hands, and his possessions have increased in the land. But now, stretch out your hand and touch all that he has, and he will surely curse you to your face." (Job 1:9-11)

So the Lord allowed Satan to take away Job's property, family, and health, but Job never cursed God or charged God with wrongdoing. Instead, he famously said, "The Lord gives and the Lord takes away; blessed be the name of the Lord" (Job 1:21).

In the next thirty-seven chapters, Job's three friends have a debate with him. They attacked and impugned Job's character and integrity, arguing that all of his suffering was from the hand of God as a result of his sin. But Job argued back that he had done no wrong and had no idea why he was being punished by God.

Finally, after a prolonged time of suffering and while arguing with his friends, the Lord spoke to Job and rebuked him. The Lord then said to Job, "Shall the one who contends with the Almighty correct him? He who rebukes God, let him answer it" (Job 40:2).

This was Job's sin. He thought it was unjust of God to allow his suffering and called into question both God's sovereignty and wisdom over the things that had transpired. Job repented and was restored. But the Lord was angry with Job's three friends. The Lord said to Eliphaz, "My wrath is aroused against you and your two friends, for you have not spoken of me what is right, as my servant Job has" (Job 42:6–7).

My point is that there are many people who do not speak what is right about the Lord God. Rather, like Job's three friends, people speak what they want to believe is true about the Lord instead of how God has disclosed himself to them. It is a serious thing to speak on behalf of the Lord and not say what is true about him.

Chapter 13

God Has Spoken to Us at Various Times and in Various Ways

> God, who at various times and in various ways spoke in time past to the fathers by the prophets, has in these last days spoken to us by his Son, whom he has appointed heir of all things, through whom also he made the worlds. (Hebrews 1:1–2)

ONE OF THE WAYS HE HAS SPOKEN TO US IS THROUGH his creation.

> The heavens declare the glory of God; and the firmament shows his handiwork. Day unto day utters speech, and night unto night reveals knowledge. There is no speech nor language where their voice is not heard. Their line has gone out through all the earth, and their words to the end of the world. (Psalm 19:1–4)

I've known people over the years who told me that they feel closest to God when they are in the mountains, in the woods, or under the starry night sky. I believe them because what they are perceiving is the created order of nature declaring God's glory. The problem with the general revelation of nature is that it merely points to God's glory. Unfortunately, this isn't enough to move people beyond complacency. What is needed is the specific revelation of the Christian scriptures, which reveal our personal responsibility to God.

The apostle Paul wrote in the New Testament, "For since the creation of the world, His (God) invisible attributes are clearly seen, being understood by the things that are made, even his eternal power and Godhead, so that they are without excuse" (Romans 1:20). General revelation, as we see here, is enough to understand several important points about God. Through nature, we can clearly see and understand that God is powerful. Through nature we can see that God is all-wise to make it all work. And, God's apparent absence in nature, tells us that God is separate and distinct from his creation. This leaves us without an excuse to pursue him further.

He has also spoken to us through past judgments. I've already addressed this through the incarceration of the fallen angels, examples of the worldwide flood, and the destruction of Sodom and Gomorrah. You will recall that some of the fallen angels had crossed a forbidden boundary for them established by God. They were then chained in the lowest depths of hell to await their final judgment. The people of the pre-flood world were destroyed because their every thought was of evil only and the resulting violence that it produced. Likewise, the people of Sodom and Gomorrah were destroyed by fire and brimstone cast down from heaven for their grave evil. All three groups await the final judgment where they will be condemned for all eternity. These past judgments of God still speak to us today.

God has also spoken to us through the temple worship of Israel.

> For this reason the Lord anciently enjoined the people of
> Israel that they should repeat the words of the priest, and

make public confession of their iniquities in the temple; because he foresaw that this was a necessary help to enable each one to form a just idea of himself.[18]

Each person should want "a just idea of himself."[19] There are people and books that can help us to a degree, but only the Lord, our creator, can help us see ourselves as we really are. The Lord instituted self-examination, confession of sin, and repentance in the Eucharist or communion services within his church, to be done on a regular basis and so that we might *form a just idea of ourselves* from the direct revelation of the Word of God.

God has spoken to us through the Jewish prophets.

> The Old Testament prophet was a proclaimer of the word, called by God to warn, exhort, comfort, teach and counsel, bound to God alone and thus enjoying a freedom that was unique.[20]

The prophet was a necessary means for God to speak to his people because the people often didn't want to hear what God had to say to them but wanted a perfunctory religion that they could perform without care or interest.

The prophet Isaiah faced this in his relationship to the people of Israel. The Lord said to him,

> Now go, write it before them on a tablet, and note it on a scroll that it may be for a time to come, forever and ever. That this is a rebellious people, lying children, children who will not hear the law of the Lord: Who say to the seers, do not see, and to the prophets, do not prophesy to us right things; speak to us smooth things, prophesy deceits. Get out of the way, turn aside from the path, Cause the holy one of Israel to cease from before us. (Isaiah 30:8–11)

This kind of rebellious response was why a prophet was essential in being able to hear directly from the Lord.

God has spoken to us through his Word, the Bible.

> All scripture [in the bible] is given by inspiration of God, and profitable for doctrine, for reproof, for correction, for instruction in righteousness, that the man of God may be complete, thoroughly equipped for every good work. (2 Timothy 3:16–17)

Here, in the biblical scriptures, we have all that we need to live in a way that is pleasing to God. A person upon whom this truth begins to dawn will quite humbly and naturally turn to the Lord, who isn't far from any of us, and seek out "instruction in righteousness" from God's Word.

Where else can we go for "reproof" [a rebuke for wrong behavior]? Usually, rebuke would come to me from a person who was an authority figure such as a parent. I never perceived any good intentions from them but only the desire that I should not give them any more grief.

Thankfully, God is a good Father who disciplines and corrects us for our own good, without which, we would descend into the popular culture that only encourages more rebellion and self-indulgence.

He will also instruct us in righteousness, which is something few people ever initiate themselves. Instruction in righteousness is an acquired taste. It doesn't come naturally to us because it deals with turning away from evil and putting to death sinful impulses and passions. Like all children, which we are spiritually, we need to be rebuked, corrected, and disciplined for wrong behavior in order to stop it. Unlike our natural fathers, who did these things to satisfy themselves, God instructs and trains us in righteousness for our own good as well.

Lastly, God has spoken to us by His Son.

> God, who at various times and in various ways spoke in time past to the fathers by the prophets, has in these last days spoken to us by his Son, whom He appointed heir of all things, through whom also he made the worlds. (Hebrews 1:1–2)

> On one occasion when many who were following the Lord were troubled by his teaching, turned away from following Christ. Jesus then turned to his twelve disciples and asked them, "Do you also want to go away? Peter answered him and said, "Lord, to whom shall we go? You have the words of eternal life?" (John 6:60–70)

Many who follow Christ share Peter's experience and observation. Like Peter, we don't understand all things with perfect clarity, but we, too, believe that Christ has "the words of eternal life."

On another day, Jesus was trying to comfort his disciples over his impending death.

> I go to prepare a place for you. And if I go to prepare a place for you, I will come again to receive you to myself; that where I am, there you may be also. And where I go you know, and the way you know. Thomas said to him, Lord, we do not know where you are going, and how can we know the way? Jesus said to him, I am the way, the truth, and the life. No one comes to the Father except through me. If you had known me, you would have known the Father also; and from now on you know him and have seen him.

> Philip said to him, Lord, show us the Father, and it is sufficient for us. Jesus said to him, have I been with you so long, and you have not known me, Philip? He who has seen me has seen the Father; so how can you say, show us

the Father? Do you not believe that I am in the Father, and
the Father in me? (John 14:1–10)

In natural theology, as I've already mentioned, affirms God's
divine status through the created order but doesn't fill in the blanks
for us. It was Christ's job to disclose the nature of God's being to us.
No one but the Son of God could reveal this to us, because only Christ
was sent by God into this world to tell us what God told him.

Isn't hearing God what we all want? He speaks to us through Christ,
his Son. Jesus said, "I have many things to say and to judge concerning
you, but he who sent me is true; and I speak to the world those things
which I heard from him" (John 8:26). On another occasion he said to
his adversaries, "But now you seek to kill me, a man who has told you
the truth which I heard from God" (John 8:40).

What distinguishes Christ from a schizophrenic? They also hear
voices, and I'm sure some who suffer these delusions claim to have
heard from God. While I'm not a psychologist, I can imagine those
who suffer from schizophrenia have lives and mental states that are
fractured with logical inconsistencies. We do not find that in Christ.
Rather, we find his thinking, reasoning, and way of life was both logical
and consistent. His life and words harmonized with the highest caliber
of morality and ethics.

But the most convincing argument for Christ being of sound
mind was that he did what only God could do. Out of compassion, he
miraculously fed thousands of people from a young boy's lunch. He
healed the sick and those with diseases, gave sight to the blind, raised
the dead to life, and, with the message of forgiveness and salvation,
liberated those who were oppressed by internal and external enemies.
These are hardly the hallmarks of a madman (see Matthew 5–9, 14, 20).

CONCLUSION

Listen Again to, "The Conclusion of the Whole Matter"

> Let us hear the conclusion of the whole matter. Fear God and keep his commandments, for this is man's all. For God will bring every work into judgment, including every secret thing, whether good or evil. (Ecclesiastes 12:13–14) (Quoted from opening statement in chapter one)

JESUS MADE THE FEAR OF GOD PALPABLE WHEN HE said, "Do not fear those who kill the body but cannot kill the soul. But rather fear him who is able to destroy both soul and body in hell" (Matthew 10:28). I hope that I've shown the distinction between the fear of God and a naïve belief that God is merely love and nothing else.

The good news is that the salvation Christ offers us is clear, straightforward, and offered to you today.

> If you confess with your mouth the Lord Jesus and believe in your heart that God raised him from the dead, you will be saved. For with the heart one believes unto righteousness, and with the mouth confession is made unto salvation. (Romans 10:9–10)

.

LIST OF SCRIPTURES

Introduction

John 3:13, 17

John 8:38, 40

Matthew 10:27–28

Chapter 1

Ecclesiastes 12:13–14

1 Chronicles 22:11–13

2 Chronicles 1:7–12

Ecclesiastes 2:4–8

Ecclesiastes 2:1–11

1 Kings 11:1–11

Ecclesiastes 7:25–26

Romans 11:29

Ecclesiastes 2:18

Romans 5:6–8

1 John 3:16

Chapter 2

2 Timothy 3:16

Psalm 119:9–11

Psalm 119:105

Luke 14:16–24

Psalm 10:3–4, 11

Ecclesiastes 8:11

2 Timothy 4:1–5

Proverbs 26:11

Chapter 3

Proverbs 1:7

Romans 1:20

Acts 14:17

Exodus 20:1–17

Matthew 22:37–40

Proverbs 6:16-19

Romans 7:19

Proverbs 16:6
Matthew 7:11
Proverbs 14:27
Proverbs 10:27
Proverbs 19:23
Proverbs 9:10–12

Chapter 4
Matthew 7:2–5
John 7:24
Matthew 12:36–37

Chapter 5
John 5:22–30
Acts 17:30–31
Hebrews 6:18
Romans 14:10–12
Philippians 2:5–11
Romans 2:6–9
Hebrews 4:12–13
Amos 5:18–20
Zephaniah 1:14–16

Chapter 6
Colossians 1:15-18
John 1:1–3
Hebrews 1:1–4
Genesis 2:7
Acts 17:24–27

Acts 17:23
Job 41:11
Psalms 89:10–11
1 Corinthians 4:5

Chapter 7
Hebrews 9:27
Hebrews 1:27
2 Corinthians 5:10
Revelation 20:11–15

Chapter 8
2 Peter 2:4–6
Acts 17:26
Jude 6
Acts 17:24–27
Matthew 8:28–32
Luke 8:31
Matthew 8:12

Chapter 9
Genesis 5
Genesis 6
Genesis 7
Genesis 8:1–19
Matthew 24:36–44

Chapter 10
Genesis 19:1–29
Ezekiel 18:23

Chapter 11

Galatians 5:19–21

Chapter 12

1 John 4:8

Job 1

Job 40:2

Job 42:6–7

Chapter 13

Hebrews 1:1–2

Psalm 19:1–4

Romans 1:20

Isaiah 30:8–11

2 Timothy 3:16–17

Hebrews 1:1–2

John 6:60–70

John 14:1–10

John 8:26

John 8:40

John 14:6

Acts 4:12

John 8:24

Romans 10:9–10

ENDNOTES

PART 1

Chapter 1

1. John MacArthur, *MacArthur Study Bible NKJV Interpretive Challenges.* Copyright 1997 Word publishing, page 925

2. Augustine, *The City of God,* 1065. Penguin Classics, Henry Bettenson, 1972, p.1065

Chapter 3

3. (*Macarthur Study Bible Historical and Theological Themes in Proverbs,* NKJV), p.874

4. Augustine, *The City of God,* 480–481.

Chapter 4

5. *Macarthur Study Bible,* footnote on Matthew 12:36

Chapter 5

6. Anselm of Canterbury, Theologians & Theology, <u>www. theologians/theology.com/God-man-</u> Anselm

Chapter 7

7. *Macarthur Study Bible,* NKJV

8. Augustine, *The City of God,* 521.

PART 2

9. *Macarthur Study Bible,* NKJV, of 2 Peter 2:4 notes

Chapter 8

10. *Macarthur Study Bible,* NKJV, footnote on Matthew 22:1.

Chapter 9

11. For a scientific account with supporting evidence see online, "Scientific Evidence for a Worldwide Flood." www. earthage.org

12. *Macarthur Study Bible,* NKJV

13. Encyclopedia of the Bible

Chapter 11

14. *New World Dictionary of American English,* third college edition 1988

15. *Pheme Perkins Interpretation Commentary on First and Second Peter, James, and Jude,* 182. John Knox press 1995

PART 3

Chapter 12

16. A.W. Tozer, *The Knowledge of the Holy: The Attributes of God: Their Meaning in the Christian Life,* 104, 105. Harper & Row 1971

17. Ibid.

Chapter 13

18. John Calvin, *The Institutes of the Christian Religion,* 543. Eerdmans Publishing 1993, translated by Henry Beverridge

19. Ibid.

20. *Dictionary of New Testament Theology,* Volume 3, 79. Zondervan 1978, Editor: Colin Brown

Made in the USA
San Bernardino, CA
05 February 2018